Animals in the Wild

Shark and Ray

by Vincent Serventy

STECK-VAUGHN
C O M P A N Y
A Subsidiary of National Education Corporation

One of the most feared sea animals is the
shark. Some kinds of sharks are

dangerous to humans. Sharks live in all of
the oceans of the world.

Different kinds of sharks range in length from six inches to sixty feet. Sharks use their sharp teeth to bite large pieces out of their prey.

The mouth of a shark is on the underside
of its head. It attacks its prey from straight
ahead. It rises above the prey and grabs it
firmly with its teeth.

Sharks have saw-like teeth that cut pieces from victims. Sharks often have rows of teeth. If a front tooth breaks off, one at the back moves up to take its place.

Sharks are scavengers. They attack and
eat sea animals that are sick or wounded.
Groups attack in feeding frenzies.
Sometimes they even eat each other.

There are hundreds of different kinds of sharks. Most are harmless to humans.

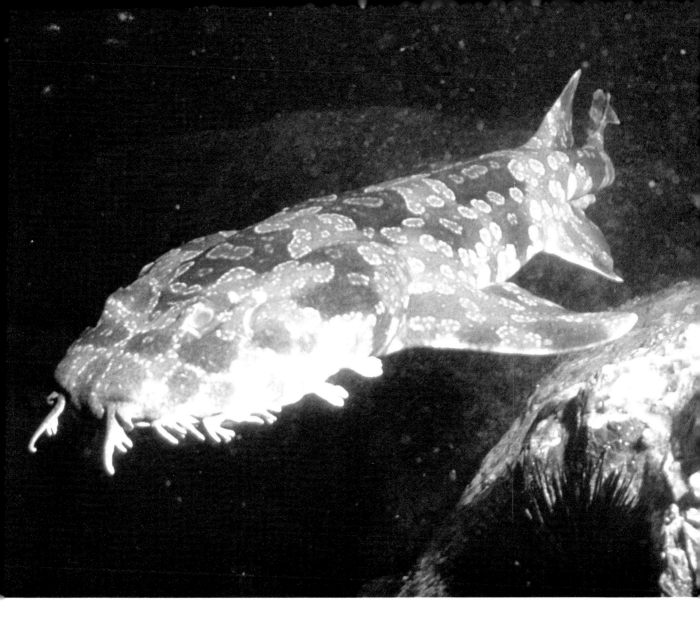

Shark scales are rough, tooth-like points.
They feel like sandpaper.

Hammerhead sharks look strange. Their eyes are on each end of the hammer.

Sharks swim very fast. They live in oceans, along seashores, and in rivers.

Bullhead, or Port Jackson, sharks have flat, heavy teeth. Their teeth can crush crabs and other hard-shelled animals. They rarely move from their places on the ocean floor.

Whale sharks are the largest of the sharks.
They grow to be sixty feet long—as large
as two elephants. They eat small animals
called plankton. Whale sharks are
harmless.

Some divers wear steel mesh suits for protection from dangerous sharks. Photographers are often lowered in cages.

Shark nets help to protect swimmers. Beaches that have nets placed offshore have fewer shark attacks.

Sharks are born ready to swim and to bite. They do not need to be cared for by their mothers. Babies taken from the bodies of mother sharks are able to swim away.

About one-third of the world's sharks lay eggs. Shark egg cases can be found on beaches. Mother sharks put the cases into cracks in reefs.

Rays are the closest relatives of sharks.
The largest of all the rays is the manta.

Manta rays are harmless. They feed on the small creatures that float in the sea.

Most rays have tails. Some of the rays are poisonous, even to humans. Most rays stay

on the ocean floor. There have been
sharks and rays for millions of years.

First Steck-Vaughn Edition 1992

First published in the United States 1985
by Raintree Publishers, A Division of Steck-Vaughn Company.

Reprinted in 1987, 1989

First published in Australia in 1984 by
John Ferguson Pty. Ltd.
133 Macquarie Street
Sydney, NSW 2000

The North American hardcover edition published by arrangement
with Gareth Stevens Inc.

Text and illustrations in this form copyright © Vincent Serventy 1984

Acknowledgments are due to Ron and Valerie Taylor for all photographs
in this book except the following:
Vincent Serventy p. 8, 18, 19.

Library of Congress number: 84-15097

Library of Congress Cataloging in Publication Data

Serventy, Vincent.
  Shark & ray.

  (Animals in the wild)
  Summary: Portrays sharks and rays in their natural surroundings and
describes their lives and struggles for survival.
  1. Sharks—Juvenile literature. 2. Rays (Fishes)—Juvenile literature.
[1. Sharks. 2. Rays (Fishes)]
I. Title. II. Title: Shark and ray. III. Series.
QL638.9.S45   1984   597'.3   84-15097

ISBN 0-8172-2402-5   hardcover library binding

ISBN 0-8114-6888-7   softcover binding

5 6 7 8 9 10 11 12 13 14   99 98 97 96 95 94 93 92

Essaye. *Try.*
Essaye encore. *Try again.*

Suis-Moi! – Follow Me!

This game of 'follow my leader' can be played with one child, or a group of children.

The leader calls out the words below one by one, and the child or children follow behind in a line, with everyone doing the actions.

The words are:

Marche! – walk

Saute! – jump

Cours! – run

Danse! – dance

Tourne! – turn

Arrête! – stop

When the leader says 'arrête!', the children have to freeze. Anyone not standing completely still, is out.

First play using English words, then once the children are used to the rules, switch to French.

Danse!

There are many types of spoken French as there are spoken English, and this
pronunciation guide is only an approximation to help you speak French with your child.
The list includes the French words for objects you see in the illustrations.
This will give you the answer to the child's question when looking at the pictures –
What's that in French? **Qu'est-ce que c'est en français?**

French	Pronunciation	English	French	Pronunciation	English
Aïe!	*i-yee*	Ouch!	**Eh!**	*eh*	Oh dear!
Arbre (l')	*arbr*	Tree	**Encore**	*on-kor*	Again
Arrête	*a-ret*	Stop	**Essaye**	*ay-ssay*	Try
Assieds-toi	*ass-yay-twa*	Sit down	**Fais voir**	*fay vwar*	Show me
Attends	*a-ton*	Wait	**Fenêtre (la)**	*fe-netr*	Window
Attention!	*a-ton-seeon*	Be careful!	**Ici**	*ee-see*	Here
Au revoir	*or rev-war*	Goodbye	**J'ai soif**	*jay swaf*	I'm thirsty
Boisson (la)	*bwa-sson*	Drink	**Je ne peux pas**	*jer ner per pa*	I can't
Bonjour	*bon-joor*	Hello	**Jouet (le)**	*joo-ay*	Toy
Bottes (les)	*bot*	Boots	**Là**	*la*	There
Ça y est	*sa ee ay*	Done it	**Léo**	*lay-oh*	Leo
C'est pour toi	*say poor twa*	This is for you	**Lève–toi**	*lev-twa*	Stand up
Chat (le)	*sha*	Cat	**Livre (le)**	*leevr*	Book
Cours	*koor*	Run	**Maison (la)**	*may-son*	House
D'accord	*da-kor'*	OK	**Marche**	*marsh*	Walk
Danse	*donss*	Dance	**Merci**	*mer-see*	Thank you
Ecoute	*ay-koot*	Listen			

French	Pronunciation	English		French	Pronunciation	English
Non	*non*	No		Tu vas où?	*tyu va oo*	Where are you going?
Où?	*oo*	Where?		Tu veux jouer?	*tyu ver joo-ay*	Do you want to play?
Oui	*wee*	Yes		Un peu	*un per*	A bit
Pauvre	*pohvr*	Poor		Viens	*vee-an*	Come
Planche à roulettes (la)	*plonsh a roo-let*	Skateboard		Voici	*vwa-see*	Here you are
Poisson (le)	*pwa-son*	Fish				
Porte (la)	*port*	Door		**The numbers from 1 to 10**		
Qu'est-ce qu'il y a?	*kess keel ya*	What's the matter?		Un	*un*	1
Rollers (les)	*ro-ler*	Rollerblades		Deux	*der*	2
Saute	*soht*	Jump		Trois	*twa*	3
Souris (la)	*soo-ree*	Mouse		Quatre	*katr'*	4
Suis-moi	*swee-mwa*	Follow me		Cinq	*sank*	5
Télévision (la)	*tay-lay-viz-yon*	Television		Six	*seess*	6
Tourne	*toorn*	Turn		Sept	*set*	7
Tu as mal?	*tyu a mal*	Have you hurt yourself?		Huit	*weet*	8
				Neuf	*nerf*	9
				Dix	*deess*	10

To Richard Dunn – O.D.
To Jessica – from Aunty Cathy

Léo le Chat Comes to Play! copyright © Frances Lincoln Limited 2003
Concept and text copyright © Opal Dunn 2003
Illustrations copyright © Cathy Gale 2003
First published in Great Britain in 2003 by Frances Lincoln Children's Books,
4 Torriano Mews, Torriano Avenue, London NW5 2RZ
www.franceslincoln.com
Distributed in the USA by Publishers Group West
British Library Cataloguing in Publication Data available on request
ISBN 0-7112-2003-4 (UK)
ISBN 1-84507-308-8 (USA)
Printed in China
1 3 5 7 9 8 6 4 2

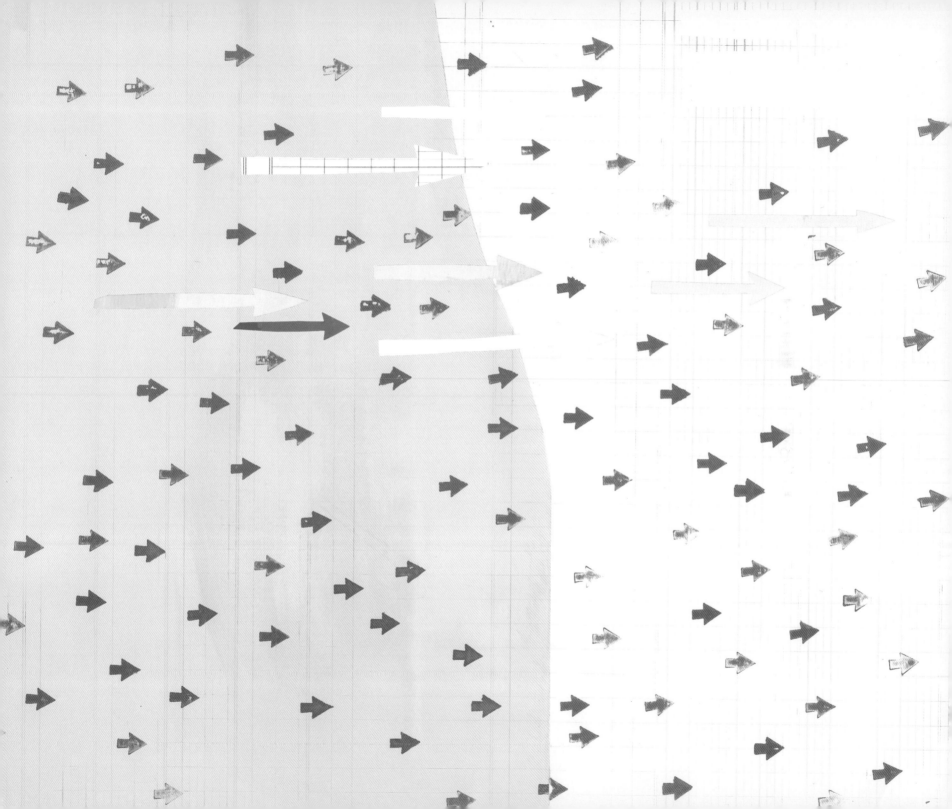

MORE BOOKS IN PAPERBACK AVAILABLE FROM FRANCES LINCOLN

El Gato Leo Comes to Play

Opal Dunn

Illustrated by Cathy Gale

Learn how to speak Spanish with El Gato Leo –
the naughty cat! Read the easy Spanish words and phrases, then lift the flap
to see the English translation.

Number Rhymes to Say and Play

Opal Dunn

Illustrated by Adriano Gon

Here are 18 lively number rhymes
and games to help your pre-school child develop and extend numeracy skills.
The colourful illustrations reinforce number concepts from 0 to 10 as well as helping
to develop language and social skills.

Frances Lincoln titles are available from all good bookshops.
You can also buy books and find out more about your favourite titles, authors and illustrators
on our website: www.franceslincoln.com